The CBCT® Teacher Guide

Center for Contemplative
Science and Compassion-Based Ethics
Emory University

Copyright © 2025 Emory University
All rights reserved.

Published by Center for Contemplative Science and
Compassion-Based Ethics, Emory University

All rights reserved. No part of this book may be reproduced, stored, or transmitted by any means—whether auditory, graphic, mechanical, or electronic—without written permission of the publisher except in the case of brief excerpts used in critical articles and reviews.
Please send inquiries to cbct@emory.edu.

Find out more at *compassion.emory.edu*

1st Edition

ISBN: 978-1-962972-14-7 (Paperback edition)

Contents

Introduction 1

PART 1: Qualities of a Teacher 3

The Three Qualities of a Teacher 5

The First Quality of a Teacher: Knowledge 6
   Studying CBCT Content 6
   Understanding CBCT Pedagogy 7
      Learning Model: The CBCT Model of Change 7
      Constructivist Approach 11
      Trauma- and Resilience-Informed Approach 12
      Co-Teaching Model 14
   What a CBCT Teacher Is and Is Not 15
   Facilitation Elements 22
      Managing the Class 22
      Leading Activities 22
      Guiding Formal Practices 22
   Fidelity and Adaptation of CBCT 38
      A Special Note on Religious and Philosophical Beliefs 39

The Second Quality of a Teacher: Practice 41
   CBCT Teacher as Learner 41

The Third Quality of a Teacher: Warm-Heartedness 43
   Applying CBCT Skills and Insights to Teaching 43

PART 2: Course Structure and Planning 53

CBCT Course Structure 55
   Component 1: Self-Guided 58

iii

    Component 2: Live Facilitation 58

Facilitation Structure of Live Sessions 59

Class Planning 62
    Guidance on Co-Teaching 62
    Teacher Preparation for Live Sessions 63
        Step 1: Engage Content and Practice 63
        Step 2: Plan the Class 64
        Step 3: Rehearse 64
        Step 4: Set Your Intention 64

Appendix A: Basic Descriptions of the Compassion Center and Its Programs 65

Appendix B: CBCT Teacher Resources 67

Introduction

This teacher guide is designed to support certified teachers of CBCT® (Cognitively Based Compassion Training) as they bring the program to their diverse communities around the world. The guide is divided into two parts. Part 1 describes the three essential qualities of a CBCT teacher: knowledge, practice, and warm-heartedness. Part 2 details key information regarding the structure and delivery of CBCT along with its e-learning platform, Compassion U™. Compassion U is a web-based app that offers full CBCT courses through a combination of self-guided activities and live facilitated sessions. The self-guided components offer the content and exercises in an interactive digital environment that includes a personal journal, meditation library, and online community. The live sessions, facilitated by a certified CBCT teacher for a group of participants (via video calls or in person), provide an opportunity for participants to dive deeper into the content and practices, receive guidance from a certified teacher, and connect with others going through the program. This guide highlights the important role of a CBCT teacher to contribute to a safe environment that supports participants' connection, exploration, and growth, and to promote the understanding and personalization of CBCT skills and insights.

PART 1
Qualities of a Teacher

The Three Qualities of a Teacher

To promote safety and compassion in the classroom environment and understanding and insight in participants, CBCT teachers cultivate the following qualities: knowledge, practice, and warm-heartedness.

These three qualities work together to support the teacher's growth and to contribute to more meaningful experiences for participants. Each quality is something we can continue to work on as we bring CBCT to others. Part 1 of this book takes a deep dive into each of these qualities, offering key information and guidance to support their cultivation. For knowledge, we review the core content of the program and unpack the essential teaching methods (i.e., pedagogy) and facilitation skills that allow this content to come to life. For practice, we focus on the important role that maintaining a personal practice plays in supporting the teaching of CBCT. For warm-heartedness, we reflect on the positive impact teachers can have when connecting to others with tenderness and acting from that place of endearment.

The First Quality of a Teacher: Knowledge

Knowledge in the context of teaching CBCT has two aspects: (1) the study of the content being delivered, and (2) the teaching methods for how to best deliver that content. A teacher needs expertise in both of these capabilities, not only to effectively share CBCT skills, insights, and practices, but also to promote a safe and compassionate space in which this knowledge can be absorbed.

In this section, we provide an overview of the core content that a CBCT teacher should be well-versed in. This content is covered in depth in the reference for all CBCT teachers, *Training Compassion: The Official Guide to CBCT®* ("the CBCT Guide"). We then take a deep dive into the pedagogy of CBCT, key facilitation elements, and a CBCT teacher's essential skills.

Studying CBCT Content

A commitment to studying and deepening understanding of CBCT's content is critical for teaching it to others. Taking a CBCT course is only a first step in this process, an introduction to the CBCT content. The Teacher Certification program is designed to then deepen that understanding. After the certification process, further commitment to familiarization is encouraged—through regularly revisiting the course activities and guide(s), engaging in Emory CBCT courses or retreats, reading published articles or research studies on CBCT, and engaging the supplemental readings provided during the teacher certification.

At a minimum, a CBCT teacher should know the following and be able to easily explain them from memory:

- **Compassion (and its "what," "why," and "how"):** Definition of compassion as it is presented in CBCT, the rationale for training compassion, and the process by which we train compassion in CBCT, along with the scientific and common-sense perspectives on this approach.

- **Emotion regulation strategies:** The three cognitive strategies for emotion regulation and how they map onto the CBCT structure.
- **Zone of Wellbeing:** The trauma- and resilience-informed model we use throughout CBCT to cultivate greater awareness of our sensations and feelings and support personal resilience.
- **Model of change:** The model of change that underlies CBCT, including the three levels of understanding and the view-familiarization-behavior model.
- **Module-specific knowledge:** For each module, this includes:
  - The official name
  - The Enduring Capabilities, how to cultivate them, and the benefits of cultivating them
  - The scientific and contemplative perspectives on the rationale for and process of cultivating the Enduring Capabilities
  - The rationale for its place in the sequence of modules (i.e., why it follows the module before it, and why it precedes the module that comes next)
  - The anchoring story
  - The insight activities and their associated takeaways
  - The formal practice steps in their assigned sequence
  - The informal practice options
  - Typical concerns participant's raise in a course and how to address them with a resilience- and trauma-informed approach

Understanding CBCT Pedagogy

Learning Model: The CBCT Model of Change

Teaching CBCT relies on the deep understanding of and ability to apply the CBCT Model of Change learning model. As we know from the CBCT Guide, the process of cultivating compassion involves integrating new views into the way we relate to the world, and we each have to take the time to make sense of these new views. However, taking on new views—even when they are more accurate and supportive of our wellbeing—does

Part 1: Qualities of a Teacher

not always happen easily or right away, especially when the new views are different from current strong or engrained views.

SUMMARY OF THE CBCT MODEL OF CHANGE

The CBCT Model of Change presents a process by which we can deepen perspectives to foster lasting and meaningful shifts over time. To fully take on a new or broader view, the model offers a step-by-step approach to move through three levels of understanding:

- **Level 1—Content Knowledge:** To reshape our views, we first need to understand them at an intellectual level. This first level of understanding comes from receiving content knowledge—hearing or reading about a new or broader view on a given topic. We gain this knowledge through activities such as reading informative books, listening to podcasts, or attending classes or talks. This level of understanding is reached when the information we receive makes logical sense to us and we are able to recall it in detail. While this is an important first step, this is insufficient to bring about changes to deeper, ingrained habits of thinking and behaving.

- **Level 2—Personalized Insight:** Personalized insight is the second level of understanding where we resonate with the knowledge and connect it to our lived experience. This is developed through critical thinking and reflective practices, including insight activities and formal analytical meditations, along with informal practices where we bring the insights into our daily lives. These practices are designed to inspire "aha" moments, connecting the content knowledge to our lived reality, and moving our understanding from the head to the heart. At this level, we experience increased meaning, motivation, and conviction, and for this reason, personalized insight has much more

Note: *Refer to the "Overview of CBCT" chapter in the CBCT Guide for additional information on this learning model.*

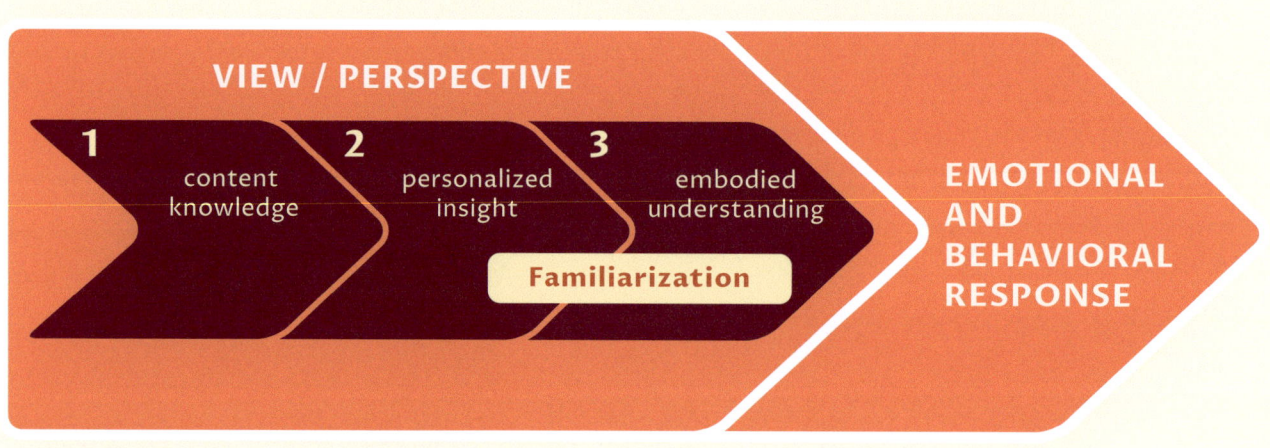

CBCT Model of Change Diagram

impact than content knowledge alone. But even so, these insights can be fleeting and in themselves may not lead to lasting changes.

- **Level 3—Embodied Understanding:** Embodied understanding is the third and final level of understanding. Here, the insights have fully soaked in and become second nature. We move toward this level by continuing the process of familiarization— examining the personalized insights from new or different angles, applying them to diverse situations, and then deliberately sustaining these insights in our awareness. This is done through formal practices that combine stabilizing and analytical meditation, along with informal practices that bring the insights into our daily lives. Embodying more realistic and helpful views leads to spontaneous, healthier emotional and behavioral responses. Through this process, desired habits become our new disposition, and unwanted habits are left behind.

Facilitating Learning at All Three Levels

As CBCT teachers, we understand that moving through the three levels of understanding allows real and lasting change to take place. It is our role to facilitate CBCT with this in mind, providing opportunities for participants to move through each level.

Facilitating at Level 1—Content Knowledge: A CBCT teacher delivers and clarifies content, making sure that concepts are clear and understood at an intellectual level. This is done by addressing questions and misunderstandings and offering further clarification and wisdom. A CBCT teacher aims to foster greater content knowledge in participants through three important avenues:

- **Common sense:** Sharing common experiences that participants can easily resonate with and understand

- **Personal experience:** Relating to the concepts using real-life examples when appropriate to illustrate or emphasize a point, especially when these examples draw on a cultural or social context that we as teachers share with participants

- **Scientific understanding:** Bringing in scientific perspectives and research to reinforce the concepts

Facilitating at Level 2—Personalized Understanding: A CBCT teacher facilitates reflective activities, practices, and discussions that are aimed at inspiring deep and personal insights in participants. A CBCT teacher encourages participants to begin applying skills and perspectives from the course into their daily lives to help deepen their understandings to this personalized level.

Facilitating at Level 3—Embodied Understanding: A CBCT teacher encourages continued and repeated practice and reflection, weaving concepts and practices into discussion throughout the course and making it clear to participants how important it is for them to do this on their own. The more frequently topics, understandings, insights, and practices are revisited, the more they are explored from different angles, and the more they are applied in life, the more embodied the understandings become. Facilitating at this level also happens when we "teach by example." Teaching by example—sometimes called modeling—occurs when a teacher has embodied the understanding through their own practice and thus models the understanding through their words or behaviors. Because embodied understanding is something that becomes second nature with practice, teachers can trust that these examples will emerge naturally from their own compassion practices over time. With the understanding of this model of change, CBCT teachers can make it clear to participants that deep habitual shifts don't happen overnight. There is a process involved—one that goes beyond a simple intellectual understanding—that relies on continued practice over time.

Each module of CBCT involves learning or reinforcing a particular skill or insight. As we move through the modules, it is important to facilitate learning at each level—to clearly present and facilitate participants' understanding of what we are cultivating, why we are cultivating it, and how we cultivate it; to provide opportunities for participants to deepen their understanding and develop insights; and to encourage the practice and application of these skills and insights.

While we understand the importance of this learning model, we also know that we cannot and should not impose anything onto our participants nor expect or promise any specific outcomes. We cannot ensure participants will move through the three levels, nor is that our goal. CBCT is an offering, and its practices are meant to be lifelong, not ones that we master in ten, a hundred, or even a thousand tries. As CBCT teachers, we aim to offer CBCT in a way that supports participants' deeper embodiment of the program's skills and insights and to let participants receive that offering in their own unique ways. We meet participants where they are and embrace the reality that each individual will take something different away from their CBCT course and develop their own relationship with the content and practices. This personal relationship is natural, and it is what makes these practices so powerful.

Constructivist Approach

As making the skills, insights, and practices personal is a core aspect of CBCT, CBCT favors a constructivist approach to teaching and learning over a straightforwardly didactic one.

A constructivist approach focuses on giving learners the resources and space to gradually come to their own conclusions and insights through a process of inquiry and discovery, rather than through passively receiving information or "correct" answers from an external authority.

Rather than explaining how things are, how they work, why they work, and how they feel, we allow participants to have those experiences first through activities, discussion, and practice. This allows learning to unfold naturally, as participants make the lessons their own. Teachers only introduce a concept to the class if and when it is needed for the participants to engage in an activity, discussion, or practice. The teacher then pulls out and weaves together the experiences and insights shared by participants to bring additional clarity to the content and practices and to correct or fill in the gaps when needed.

As CBCT teachers, we attempt to prioritize the learning needs and inquiry processes of our participants as they arise, rather than rigidly focusing on reaching our own preconceived goals. Part of the power of CBCT experiences is that they rely on and encourage personal inquiry, exploration, and reflection. Rather than leading participants to preordained responses or points of view, the course activities include a variety of approaches—engaging in mindful and respectful dialogue and active listening, applying critical thinking, and using perspective-taking skills—to allow participants to come to their own understanding of the material.

While we might feel the urge to steer participants firmly or quickly toward the specific understandings of the material that we deem most important or true, it's best to resist that urge. Participants will gain more from their CBCT experiences if they are supported in using their skills in questioning, observing, hypothesizing, and discerning. In this way, participants will come to their own critical insights and "aha" moments, allowing them to connect more authentically to the subject matter and decide what is most true and useful for their lives.

When participants express insights or offer challenging questions as they explore CBCT, a CBCT teacher may consider allowing and celebrating these insights, even if they do not initially correspond to the teacher's personal beliefs, opinions, or experiences with CBCT. Such openness will encourage a spirit and atmosphere of exploration and questioning, an essential attitude for any CBCT practitioner. This approach is especially important when considering questions of emotions, relationships, and values, which can be deeply personal.

As CBCT teachers, we trust in the process of exploration and the power of insight activities and the formal and informal practices to allow participants to internalize their insights and cultivate an increased awareness of the choices they have to support their wellbeing. We trust the participants' self-agency.

Trauma- and Resilience-Informed Approach

CBCT takes a trauma- and resilience-informed approach, primarily through its alignment with and incorporation of the insights and skills of the Community Resilience Model (CRM), developed by trauma expert and director for the Trauma Resource Institute, Elaine Miller-Karas.

Trauma is an individual's response to events that they perceive as overwhelmingly challenging, such as poverty, exposure to violence, abuse, oppression, natural disasters, and illness.[1] Although trauma is ubiquitous, many teachers are often unaware of what their participants have experienced. As the saying goes, "We don't have to know the story to know that there is a story."

To be *trauma-informed* is to be guided by an understanding of how stress and trauma impact individuals' and communities' emotional and physical lives, learning, and wellbeing. CBCT relies on trauma-informed pedagogy, which includes creating a learning environment that supports a sense of belonging and promotes individual and collective resilience.

CBCT incorporates the latest developments in trauma research and trauma-informed care for teachers and participants to explore emotions, self-regulation, and reflective practices safely and effectively. This involves the inclusion of the following CRM practices in the "Overview" and "Getting Started" chapters of the CBCT Guide:

Note: *For more information on the CRM practices: refer to the "Overview of CBCT" and "Getting Started" chapters of the CBCT guide.*

- Grounding
- Tracking
- Resourcing

---

1 Miller-Karas, E. (2015). *Building Resilience to Trauma: The Trauma and Community Resiliency Models*. New York: Routledge.

- Shift and Stay
- "Help Now!" Strategies

The Help Now! Strategies are also presented as the informal practices in the Overview module of the Training Compassion course in Compassion U. The CRM practices all involve attuning to body sensations and they provide participants with immediate tools for dealing with stress that can be used daily, thereby reducing hyper- and hypo-activity and helping them be better prepared for learning. All people go through experiences that can be perceived as scary or threatening, so participants of CBCT need not have suffered from serious or "big T" trauma (although some will have) to benefit from practices that involve attending to the body and sensations. These tools serve as an important foundation for the subsequent cultivation of self-regulation, interpersonal, and systems skills covered in the CBCT modules.

A greater awareness of sensations, which can be cultivated through practice, can help us to realize when our bodies are in a state of wellbeing—what Miller-Karas calls the zone of resilience or the Zone of Wellbeing (ZOW). Similarly, we can start to notice more quickly when we are out of that zone, either due to hyper-arousal (overwhelming anxiety, anger, or agitation) or hypo-arousal (lethargy, feeling depressed). This awareness is the first step in learning to balance the body and return to a state of physiological wellbeing, which is a precondition for acting in the best interest of oneself and others.

CBCT's *resilience-informed* approach is a strengths-based approach to learning that recognizes that everyone has some level of resilience that has allowed them to survive in the face of life's stressors and traumas, and which can be strengthened further with knowledge and practice. CBCT focuses on building strengths and capabilities rather than focusing on remedying deficits. The skills and insights strengthened in CBCT can help participants who have experienced trauma develop a sense of control and competence. Those same skills can prepare participants who have been less impacted by trauma to be more prepared to face challenges that lie ahead.

Beyond incorporating information about the nervous system, ZOW, and CRM practices, CBCT content, practices, and teachers take a trauma- and resilience-informed approach through:

- Strengths-based practices and language
- Development of resilience skills and self-compassion

Note: *Since experts advise that even just noticing and attending to body sensations can lead to a reactivation of past trauma, it is highly recommended that the tracking practice be taught together with other practices, such as grounding and resourcing.*

- Invitational language (never forcing any action or insisting on one approach)
- Offering of multiple options in activities
- Live sessions that provide a source of safety, kindness, and compassion
- Normalization of a wide variety of experiences
- Respect for diverse identities, ways of thinking, beliefs, backgrounds, and personalities
- Non-judgmental language (that involves not making assumptions about people's views or experiences)

Note: *Specific guidance on how to incorporate these elements into teaching and facilitation is provided on pages 24–37 of this guide.*

Co-Teaching Model

CBCT encourages a co-teaching model for CBCT. While not required, having two teachers to facilitate courses and workshops is a model that is designed to enhance the experience for both teachers and learners. This can be especially helpful in the first few years of teaching CBCT. Co-teaching can help in the following ways:

Diverse perspectives: Co-teachers might bring in different perspectives on the content itself or different strategies and approaches to the practices. This is beneficial because a variety of perspectives on the CBCT modules can deepen learning in participants and teachers. For teachers, it can allow them to look at things in a new way, gain greater insights, and help avoid having a rigid or fixed stance. Teachers, after all, are learners too—our growth and learning doesn't stop! Diverse perspectives can also provide participants with a greater opportunity to connect with the material and practices. If they don't resonate with one view, they may resonate with another.

Different strengths: Every CBCT teacher has their own unique strengths. Some of us may be more comfortable with facilitating activities, some with guiding meditation, some with delivering content, some with sharing personal experiences, and some with presenting science. Having access to more strengths between two teachers makes a better experience for the learners. It also gives the teachers an opportunity to learn from their co-teacher's strengths, and even a safety net to experiment with elements of the teaching they are less comfortable with, knowing that they have their co-teacher there to support them.

More opportunity for connection: Co-teaching gives participants the opportunity to connect with two teachers instead of one. In some cases, participants may not connect with their CBCT teacher, which may lead them to drop the course altogether and miss the opportunity to engage in the experience. Having two teachers provides a greater chance that the participants will connect with at least one of them. Co-teaching also gives teachers the opportunity to develop a new connection with each other or strengthen an existing one through the experience.

Having someone to lean on: Sometimes things come up in our lives, and if a teacher is unable to give their full attention to the planning or the facilitation of a class, they have someone to support them in that moment and make sure the participants can continue their learning with someone they know and have already developed a connection with. Having someone to lean on is also important in moments when teachers will inevitably lose attention, forget information, say something wrong, or not know how to respond to a question or handle a situation.

Accountability: Having a co-teacher often reinforces a sense of accountability when teaching, when it comes to planning for the class and staying on course. This helps teachers avoid leaving things to the last minute. It also helps to have accountability when planning and thinking things through with the class, putting together a meaningful experience, getting back to focus in class when tangents or distractions come up, or having the co-teacher jump in to help when a teacher has forgotten or deviated from the plan in an unhelpful way.

Note: *Go to "Guidance on Co-Teaching" on page 62 for more specific information and guidelines on co-teaching.*

Modeling: Co-teachers are able to model the skills and qualities cultivated in CBCT with each other in the class setting. This gives the teachers the chance to put those skills and qualities into practice and deepen their own embodiment of them and enhances the learning and growth of the participants experiencing and witnessing that themselves.

What a CBCT Teacher Is and Is Not

CBCT Does Not Dictate Behavior

CBCT does not prescribe or provide individualized answers to problems. When teaching CBCT, we do not take on the roles of mentors, friends, or family members—our role is not to give our opinions on personal situations or to solve the issues that our participants face and may bring up during the course.

As CBCT teachers, we facilitate the process for participants to engage in their own reflection, learning, and discernment. CBCT offers practices to strengthen skills and tools, but then it is in the hands of the participants themselves. We don't tell them what to do with those tools or assume that there is one right answer.

CBCT Is Not a Fix-All

We want to make it clear to our participants that CBCT is not a "fix-all" program. It provides practices that we believe can support our lives, but it is not going to fix all of our problems, and it is up to each individual whether they find the program useful and want to continue.

CBCT Teachers Are Guides on the Side

We can understand our role in many ways as being a "guide on the side, not a sage on the stage." Similar to mindfulness programs, CBCT "is not group therapy. It is not psychoeducation. And it is not classroom teaching. All the 'group-work skills' can be seen, rather, as rooted in the co-creation . . . among teachers and participants."[2] While trained to teach CBCT, CBCT teachers are not all-knowing experts. We too are learning and growing, on our own and with our participants. The learning and growth that emerges in the course is a group effort—facilitated by the teacher, but achieved by the group as a whole. This depends on our ability to take a step back from the more didactic approach to teaching and lean into the constructivist approach (discussed on page 11). Our role as both teacher and learner is discussed further in "The Second Quality of a Teacher: Practice" section on page 41.

CBCT Training Is Not Professional Mental Health Training

Our role as certified CBCT teachers is to contribute to a safe space for our participants and offer practices that can support their wellbeing. It is important to be mindful that CBCT teacher training does not give us the qualifications of a mental health professional or licensed practitioner, and although some CBCT teachers hold these credentials, they are not expected to function in that role when teaching CBCT.

CBCT is trauma- and resilience-informed, but this does not guarantee that participants will never experience dysregulation during a course. CBCT includes a set of practices that involve turning the attention inward,

---

2 McCown, D., Reibel, D., & Micozzi, M. S. (2010). The skills of the teacher. In *Teaching Mindfulness*. New York: Springer. https://doi.org/10.1007/978-0-387-09484-7_5

recalling memories, and working with sensations, feelings, and thoughts, and practices that involve working with our perception of others. In some cases, these practices may lead to feelings of distress, dysregulation, or activation. Individuals might also experience strong emotions outside of their ZOW during group sharing, associated with being activated or offended by something shared. Group sharing might also reveal a past or current trauma or abuse being faced by a participant.

Please refer to the following section for guidance on how to respond to challenging situations when someone appears dysregulated or activated in a live CBCT session.

Part 1: Qualities of a Teacher

Guidance on How to Respond to Challenging Situations

In moments when someone appears dysregulated or activated, reports distress, or there is concern for a participant's safety or wellbeing, it is not our role to act as a mental health professional. What we *can* do in those moments is:

1. **Pause.** Stop and breathe to give everyone a chance to attune to their settling or grounding practices. Use this pause to consider whether you need to continue the activity as you had envisioned it. Be open to changing plans. Make eye contact with your co-teacher, if you have one, to give them permission to step in, as sometimes, when you are at a loss, the other person sees a way forward.

2. **Acknowledge the reality of the emotion and—if possible—normalize it.** This is an opportunity to engage your non-judgmental awareness, allowing the situation and the emotions to be what they are in the moment before you react or try to control or fix the situation. Sometimes the situation is so intense, or changing so quickly, that taking the time to pause to determine the best response will require accepting the difficult situation for what it is, relying on the Module 3 self-awareness skills.

   > **Example**: In one class of 30 people, after the first nurturing moment practice, many people shared how wonderful they felt. Then, one participant raised their hand and said, with a somber voice, "I have just realized that I have never felt safe in my entire life." The room went silent as this participant held eye contact with the teacher, searching for an answer. After a breath, the teacher nodded slightly and said quietly, "You are not alone." The teacher paused some more, attuning to the sensations of the moment. Looking around the room, heads were nodding, so the teacher said, "I see heads nodding," and turned back to connect with the participant. (Making visible the reality that people are not alone in their difficult experiences is sometimes called "normalizing.") Slowly, the teacher began to present the CBCT content, noting that there are many alternatives to working with nurturing moments when they don't come to mind or when emotions are difficult. However, the teacher did not move on to this content before taking plenty of time to acknowledge the reality of the difficult emotion or experience.

3. **Acknowledge the teacher's error, if there is one**. In some cases, a teacher's words or actions may cause pain. If you become aware that this has happened, we recommend that you do your best not to take it personally, get defensive, or blame others. In these moments, it is helpful to pause and acknowledge the real feelings of others (see Point 2 above). In cases where the teacher realizes they have made a mistake, they may choose to acknowledge that mistake and apologize, if it feels genuine to do so. Teachers may also choose to respond by letting the participants know they will think about what happened and get back to them with a follow-up statement or plan to address that hurt. These situations are wonderful opportunities to illustrate the self-compassion premise that, though we all make mistakes, we are not a mistake.

4. **Shift the class dynamic in a significant way.** Sometimes a whole class can be derailed by a comment that is shocking or upsetting. After pausing and assessing the situation, you may realize that the best option is to move on and not bring too much emphasis to the person or people at the center of the commotion. They may be embarrassed or have shut down and turned inward, so it does not make sense to focus on them. One way to shift this focus is to shift the activity to something very different—perhaps moving on to a new topic altogether or saying that it seems to be time for a settling practice, a standing stretch, or even a 10-minute break to get some water, walk outside, or visit the toilet.

5. **Follow up with the person, one-on-one.** It is important to remember that CBCT is not a trauma-processing group, and that we as teachers are able to remind participants that we are focusing on building the CBCT skills outlined in each module. If a participant seems to be struggling with strong emotions or they share information that makes you concerned for their safety or wellbeing, we request that CBCT teachers reach out to the individual (before or after class) to check in on their wellbeing and ensure they have adequate access to resources and support. We have a list of mental health support contact information that can be shared with participants (see page 21). This does not include a list of specific providers. It is at the teacher's discretion if they would like to connect a participant with a list of potential providers.

> **Example 1:** Participant seems activated in class. They are visibly upset and crying after someone else in the group shared a vulnerable story. Teacher notices the participant

is still upset after class and they leave abruptly. Teacher decides to email the participant later that day.

- *Teacher email*: "Dear [participant name], I noticed you were upset in class today, and I wanted to reach out to make sure you are okay and to see if something came up in the class that would be helpful for me to address."

- *Participant response:* "Thank you so much for reaching out to check in on me. Nothing you need to address. Someone brought up a story in class today that activated me. I am okay now. Just needed a minute to reset."

- *Teacher response:* "I am glad to hear you are okay. Please let me know if there are any resources I can share for any further support."

- *Participant response:* "I am doing okay now but thank you."

Example 2: A participant mentions that they are experiencing increasingly hard-to-manage mental health symptoms. After class, the teacher emails the participant:

- *Teacher email*: "Hey there, I am reaching out to connect about what you shared in class today regarding your mental health."

- *Participant does not respond*. Teacher waits until the night before the next class, and when there is still no response, sends a follow-up email.

- *Teacher second email attempt:* "You had mentioned your mental health being a struggle right now and that you are experiencing some challenges managing that. I wanted to check in to make sure you are safe and okay. I am also including a list of providers you can reach out to if you need additional support."

Example 3: A participant alludes to the fact that they are experiencing abuse at home when sharing in the group. After class, the teacher pulls the person aside. (Note: In a situation like this, it is best to avoid sending an email to the participant, for safety reasons).

- *Teacher*: "Do you have a minute to talk?"

The First Quality of a Teacher: Knowledge

- *Participant*: "Yes."

- *Teacher*: "I want to thank you for sharing with me and the group today. When you said _____, it made me a little concerned for your safety. I wanted to check in with you to see how you feel about your own safety and if you would be interested in connecting with a mental health provider. I am so glad you are a part of our CBCT class, and I want to make sure I can support you through this experience and what might be coming up for you."

- *Participant*: "I am safe, but this has been a really challenging situation. If you could help connect me to someone, that would be great."

- *Teacher:* "Of course. What is the best way for me to contact you to share a list of mental health resources?"

6. **Contact the CBCT team.** If a participant in your class has a strong or concerning reaction during the course, you are welcome to reach out to the CBCT team for additional consultation and guidance on how to best respond. (Consider reaching out to the person who served as your supervisor for guidance.)

7. **Remember the Out of ZOW button.** Remind participants that the Compassion U platform has an Out of ZOW button with resource links for participants who feel dysregulated, including:

    - "Help Now!" Strategies
    - Settling practices
    - Contact information for mental health support (also listed below)

Mental Health Helplines https://www.helpguide.org/find-help.htm

Crisis Centres and Helplines—IASP https://www.iasp.info/crisis-centres-helplines/

Helplines, Suicide Hotlines, and Crisis Lines from around the World https://www.therapyroute.com/article/helplines-suicide-hotlines-and-crisis-lines-from-around-the-world

Suicide Hotlines and Prevention Resources around the World https://www.psychologytoday.com/us/basics/suicide/suicide-prevention-hotlines-resources-worldwide

Facilitation Elements

The main facilitation elements that we engage in when teaching CBCT include, managing the class, leading activities, and guiding formal practices (meditations). When going through the various facilitation elements of a class, we bring the intention with us to hold a safe and compassionate space and to promote understanding and insight. As we walk through what each of these elements entails in a CBCT class, we will also begin to unpack the skills of the teacher that help us facilitate and support the CBCT experience of participants.

Managing the Class

A CBCT teacher is responsible for setting expectations and creating and managing the class agenda. Setting expectations involves clarifying what a CBCT course and teacher are and are not (refer to page 15 for this list). It involves giving participants an idea of the sessions' format and what is expected of them between sessions. Managing the class also involves making sure the class flows in a meaningful way. At times, this will involve stepping in to stay on course with the plan, and at other times, it will involve making changes on the spot. "Skills for Managing the Class" can be found on page 24.

Leading Activities

Because of our constructivist approach to CBCT, activities are at the heart of teaching and facilitation. Rather than diving into lectures telling participants how things work and what things feel like, we allow them the opportunity to experience it for themselves. We then we work together to unpack those experiences. Activities also provide opportunities for participants to learn from and connect with each other through sharing and discussion. "Skills for Leading Activities" can be found on page 26.

Guiding Formal Practices

Each CBCT module focuses on specific skills or insights, and each has their own unique formal practice designed to train those particular capabilities. Participants may come to the live session already familiar with that module's practice. In some cases, they may have tried it just once or twice on their own. In other cases, participants may come to the session never having experienced it. A CBCT teacher is able to set up, guide, and unpack the practice, regardless of participants' prior experience, or lack thereof. "Skills for Guiding Meditation" can be found on page 33.

SKILLS FOR
Managing the Class

Sets expectations

A CBCT teacher sets expectations about the class and the roles of the teacher and participants at the beginning of a course and throughout.

- ✓ "I'm going to step in at times to keep us on track. I will be setting time parameters, and may interrupt in some cases."

- ✓ Expectations can be set through the facilitation of **"Group Intentions"** (sometimes referred to as a "Group Agreement"). The goal of this exercise is to co-create a set of intentions to support an environment of safety, support, and learning throughout a CBCT course. Teachers will often present a list of items in the first session, which might include:

  - Keeping what is shared in group discussions confidential
  - Being mindful that all have an equal opportunity to speak or ask questions
  - Assuming best intentions in others
  - Respecting different views and beliefs
  - Staying present

  The teacher can then invite the participants to alter or add items to the list that they feel would support their experience and the experience of others. The teacher can write all the points on a whiteboard or a slide, mentioning that the group can return to this list at any time to review and update it. The teacher may even choose to review this list at the start of each class.

Manages time well

A CBCT teacher is responsible for managing time well. This involves planning a realistically timed agenda, starting and ending on time, keeping track of time throughout the session, and steering the group when needed to move onto other important agenda items.

- ✓ "This is a very interesting discussion, but in the interest of time . . . "; "I'm sorry to cut this off, but it's time for us to move into the next activity . . . "; "To make sure we have time for our practice, let's shift now to . . ."

Makes changes on the spot

Flexibility is an important skill of a CBCT teacher—adjusting the agenda when timing goes differently than expected or when a shift would help to meet the needs of the group. This might happen due to a struggle, misunderstanding, or vulnerability brought up in the group that would benefit from more discussion time before moving on to the next activity. It might even involve discarding something on the agenda in order to do so or changing the structure or timing of it.

- ✓ "Thank you for bringing up this important point. Let's take some time now to unpack this before we move on to the next activity"; "Instead of moving into the next activity, let's spend more time on this topic"; "Would it be helpful for you all if we spend more time on this instead of moving on to the next activity?"

SKILLS FOR

Leading Activities

Setting Up the Activity

Orients participants to what they are about to engage in

Activities often need some setup. For some activities, this can be a simple and brief introduction to give the participants a sense of what they are about to do. Providing information about the focus of the activity, how long the activity will be, and whether it will include personal reflection and/or sharing can alleviate the anxiety that can arise for some when they are not sure what is coming next.

> ✓ "In this next activity, 'Connecting through Our Shared Human Condition,' we're going to explore how we categorize people as we go about our lives and we'll reflect upon the effects of that categorization. We'll spend about five minutes journaling on specific prompts and then we will put you into small groups of three or four people for about 10 minutes where you will be invited to share any reflections or insights, if you are comfortable doing so. We will then come back to the large group to debrief."

Knows when to deliver content and when to jump right in

In some cases, the setup will require delivering content; however, to stick with our constructivist approach, it is important to *only* deliver content that is absolutely necessary for the participant to engage in the activity. We can ask ourselves: What do they really need to know in order to do this activity? If the activity is about the ZOW, for example, we would need to explain that concept. Or, if we are asking participants to think about heedfulness, we would need to define that term. But other activities can be done without first receiving content, like the "Talking to a Friend" activity in Module 4. In those cases, we can jump right in.

> ✓ **Delivering content:** "We will now engage in an activity called 'What's at Stake?', where we'll explore the quality of heedfulness, which is a heightened sense of care, motivation, and careful attention. This quality can arise when we understand what's at stake if we're not attentive. This activity is about making visible what's at stake so we can cultivate the heedfulness that will help us stay focused on what really matters to us."

- ✓ **Jumping in:** "To kick off this module, we will start with an activity called 'Talking to a Friend.'"

Gives clear instructions

The setup also involves giving clear instructions for the activity, in short segments and a step-by-step manner. Written instructions are often helpful. It is important to repeat instructions several times to ensure everyone has heard them and they are clear. It can also be helpful to check in with participants, even having them re-state the instructions to ensure everyone has understood before beginning the activity.

- ✓ "Again, we will be going into breakout rooms for eight minutes. Each person will have two minutes to share. You will then have five minutes to discuss as a group and come up with one to three themes that emerged from the sharing, and any insights or questions that came up. These instructions have also been shared in the chat for your reference. Any questions before we begin?"

Remains trauma- and resilience-informed

It is important when starting any activity, practice, or discussion that we remain trauma- and resilience-informed and use invitational language, inviting, not forcing, participants to engage in the activity, and giving alternate options. We want to remind people that these practices are for *them*. If something doesn't feel right for them at a certain time, that is okay.

- ✓ "If you feel comfortable . . . "; "I invite you to . . . "; "You can write, draw, or just think about . . . "; "You can imagine or reflect on something less personal if you choose . . ."

- ✗ "This is a journaling exercise, so everyone write out your answers."

Part 1: Qualities of a Teacher

Reflection

Holds space for individual reflection

A CBCT teacher provides adequate wait-and-think time when asking questions. It is always helpful and advised to give participants time to reflect on their own before sharing in groups. Even 30 seconds to reflect on a prompt or to journal can give people time to put their thoughts together and then engage in more meaningful sharing.

- ✓ "Does anyone need another minute to finish up their personal reflection?"; "We'll take about another 30 seconds, so you can begin wrapping up your thoughts."

Holds space for group reflection

Note: If using slides when teaching online, please don't leave the slides up when sharing is taking place. Taking the slides off the screen allows the participants to see each other while they share, making it easier to connect.

Often, what helps to deepen understanding and inspire new insights and realizations is group discussion. This also promotes connection and that sense of safety that uplifts the experience of the participant. This can be done in small or large groups, or some combination thereof. But again, everything in CBCT is optional. We want to make sure people know that there are different ways of sharing, and that they can choose to not share at all.

- ✓ "We will now put you into small groups to continue this reflection. You are welcome to share the situation you reflected on or just an insight, takeaway, or question that came up. You are also welcome to keep your reflections to yourself and be a listener in the group."

- ✗ "We will now put you into small groups where everyone will take a turn sharing what they reflected on with each other."

Debrief and Takeaway

Uses language that is open and non-presumptive

It is important that CBCT teachers do not make assumptions or say things definitively that may not be true for everyone. Regardless of our personal experiences or beliefs, it is important that we remain open and withhold from making claims.

- ✓ "CBCT offers practices that aim to alleviate stress."

- ✗ "CBCT will reduce your stress levels."

Asks open-ended questions

Asking open-ended questions helps to stimulate critical and reflective thinking and encourages sharing, allowing participants to discover their own key insights and takeaways.

- ✓ "What did you notice while doing that activity?"; "Describe any feelings or sensations that came up."; "What insights or questions arose for you during that activity?"

- ✗ "Did you enjoy this exercise?"; "Does everyone understand?"

Knows when to listen, when to let others respond, and when to jump in and respond

A CBCT teacher maintains a healthy balance between sitting back to allow for participants' reflections and dialogue with each other and jumping in to respond to comments, situations, and questions. Sometimes, the teacher will jump in to reinforce or clarify content in the middle of the discussion. In other cases, the teacher will listen and let everyone share before responding, then will bring up and emphasize key points in a final takeaway that wraps up the activity. It could also be done in both ways: jumping in during the discussion and providing a wrap-up at the end. This is up to the teachers and what they feel is needed for the class at that time.

Some things to consider would be:

- How much have you, as the teacher, talked already?
- Is this a good time to take a step back and allow other voices to come in without interjecting?
- Is this a good opportunity for the participants to make sense of the content through sharing and learn from each other? Or is it a good opportunity to jump in to address questions and misunderstandings?
- Is this a good time for the participants to connect with each other?
- Did something really off-base or sensitive arise that needs to be responded to more immediately?

Uses active listening and non-judgmental language to gain clarity on what participants are sharing and affirm differences of opinions and responses from the group

CBCT participants come to the program with their unique perspectives and experiences, some of which may not resonate with our own or with those of others in the group. A CBCT teacher uses active listening to take in what the group has to say, asks clarifying questions when needed, and refrains from highly praising learner responses so as not to show preference for certain responses over others. The teacher acknowledges the wide array of experiences, opinions, and responses.

- ✓ "What I think I hear you saying is . . . "; "Thank you for sharing"; "I appreciate hearing the variety of thoughts on this topic"; "These are all interesting points to consider"; "I'm not sure about that. Does someone else have a thought about this?"

- ✗ "What you're saying is . . . "; "I don't understand how this relates to the topic"; "That's not right."

Reinforces and clarifies content and redirects the class when a participant or group is going off-topic

A CBCT teacher is responsible for listening to the group as they share ideas, pulling out the key points from the discussion, summarizing important points made by learners, or asking clarifying questions if needed. A CBCT teacher provides time for, and is responsive to, questions from learners and can address confusion and fill in gaps if important content was not mentioned in the sharing. There will be moments while teaching CBCT when an individual or the group brings up a topic that is not related to the class or the intended focus at that time. In those moments, a CBCT teacher may need to redirect the class to the topic of focus, like the gentle, attentive trainer of the elephant, guiding the elephant back to the post. When redirecting, try to find something in what they've said that does or could be tied back to the topic, if possible.

- ✓ "This is great, thank you for sharing. What I hear that is so important in this sharing is [insert something about what they were saying that touches on the module to redirect them]"; "This was a great discussion, thank you all for sharing. I'd like to offer another reflection on this module . . . "

- ✗ "This is off topic"; "We have to get back on track."

Example from a Module 3 class:

- *Participant:* "When I struggle, what I like to do is just take deep breaths and connect with the inner spirit. I used to react all the time to everything that came up, but this has really helped me to stop reacting so quickly."

> ༄ ***Teacher***: "That's wonderful. It is true that taking moments to pause and breathe can have such a powerful impact when it comes to settling. You are also highlighting a really important skill that we work to strengthen in this module: the ability to pause in the midst of a stressful situation. In the case of Module 3, we learn to pause and observe non-judgmentally so as not to get entangled with what is coming up and, like you mentioned, we learn to respond instead of react. As Viktor Frankl says, 'Between stimulus and response there is a space. In that space is our power to choose our response. In our response lies our growth and our freedom.' Thank you so much for bringing up this important point."

Pays attention to the group's dynamics and learners' energy, attention levels, comprehension, and emotions

Being able to sense energy levels, feelings, and understanding in the group allows the teacher to better understand and respond to the needs of the group or of specific individuals. To do this, a teacher can pause and ask participants to reflect on their own attention levels, emotions, and sensations throughout the course. The teacher can observe the facial expressions and body language of participants to notice their levels of engagement and distraction. A teacher can then respond by bringing in energizing activities or breaks, as needed, or offering clarification.

> ✓ "To settle into the class, let's take a few deep breaths"; "Let's take a few minutes to stand up and stretch, moving the body to bring in more energy!"; "We'll take a five-minute break. Please feel free to grab some tea or water and take a breather before we dive back in."

Attunes to participant engagement and provides opportunities for all voices to be heard

In cases where some participants seem less engaged in discussions and sharing, this could be due to those participants' style of processing information or their personal comfort levels. In other cases, individuals in the group might dominate or take over. A CBCT teacher is alert to participation inequalities within the group, makes space for quieter voices, and stops someone from speaking too long or derailing a conversation.

> ✓ "Is there anyone who hasn't spoken yet that would like to add something?"

Manages challenging situations

A CBCT teacher is able to respond to challenging situations that emerge in the class, particularly difficult emotions or reactions that come up in response to an activity or sharing. Please refer to "Guidance on How to Respond to Challenging Situations" on page 18.

Summarizes key points clearly and succinctly

A CBCT teacher serves as a "guide on the side" as participants reflect on and share their personal experiences and insights. That being said, a CBCT teacher is also responsible for and able to clearly synthesize key takeaways and must be able to wrap up an activity.

- ✓ "As we've seen in this activity, there are countless others we depend on daily for even one object. Keeping this in mind can transform the way we think of, feel about, and engage with others in our lives. As many of you highlighted in your sharing, reflecting on the Web of Interdependence gives us the opportunity to feel gratitude, tenderness, and warmth for an ever-widening circle of beings. And it's this warm-hearted connection that is central to compassion."

SKILLS FOR

Guiding Meditation

Setting Up the Practice

Orients participants to what they are about to engage in

Similar to activities, formal practices need some set up, even if it is brief. To prepare participants for the practice, it is helpful to orient them to the basics of the practice, specifically, the general steps they can expect, how long the practice will be, whether they will hear a bell at the start and end, etc.

> ✓ "We will now engage in the Module 1 formal practice. We'll guide you through it, step by step. In the Module 1 formal practice, you'll be asked to spend some time immersing yourself in your chosen moment of nurturance and reflecting on its benefits, as you have already begun doing in the insight activities. Feel free to use one of the moments you've already thought of or pick a new one if it comes to mind. Each practice can be viewed as an experiment, so please do keep checking in with yourself throughout the practice and adjust as needed for you to do what feels right for you. The practice will last for eight minutes. You will hear a bell at the start and end. Before we start, please take a moment to stretch and reposition your body as much as you wish."

Gives them time to choose what they will reflect on in the practice, when appropriate.

It is helpful to give participants time to choose what they will reflect on in the practice. Often, the insight activities have participants reflect on situations or insights that they can bring back into their practice, meaning they will not need much time (or any at all) to prepare beforehand. In other cases, they may need some time to consider what they want to work with in the practice before they begin.

> ᔆ For example, having them reflect on a nurturing moment before engaging in the Module 1 practice, choosing which object of focus they want to use as an anchor for the Module 2 practice, having time to think about the difficult situation they want to reflect on for the Module 4 practice, or the three individuals in the close, neutral, and difficult categories for the Module 6 practice.

Knows when to offer guidance on common struggles with the practice.

The setup provides an opportunity for the teacher to give any tips or guidance on common struggles that would be helpful to address before diving into the practice.

- For example, for the Module 2 practice, it is helpful to remind practitioners before they begin that the mind will wander away from the chosen object of focus, and that this is actually a key part of the practice. Each time we notice and bring the attention back, we strengthen our skill of attention.

We do, however, want to be careful not to label something as challenging before participants have come to that conclusion for themselves.

- For example, in the Module 7 practice, some people experience feelings of anger or guilt when they reflect on interdependence, as it makes them more aware of injustice and others' suffering. This is not the case for everyone, nor does it come up in every class. This is an example of something that would be better not to bring up prior to the practice. If it comes up in the debrief, it could be addressed at that point.

Remains trauma- and resilience-informed

We remain trauma- and resilience-informed by inviting, not forcing, participants to engage in the practice. We want to remind people that these practices are for them. If something doesn't feel right for them at a certain time, that is okay. We give them the choice to follow our guidance as we lead the meditation, to tune us out and self-guide if that is more helpful for them, to stay with another practice that feels more important for them to engage in in that moment, or to stop altogether if that is what feels right for them.

- ✓ "If this feels uncomfortable at any time in the formal practice, you can think of situations that are not as raw or activating. You can also always return to any of the earlier practices or stop altogether"; "This practice is for *you*, so please follow what feels best for you during the practice. You may choose to follow the guidance or to tune it out and guide yourself, please do what feels right."

Guidance

The list below is a helpful reference for guiding formal practices:

- **Finding your voice:** It can help to find a balance between guiding with a calm, steady, and clear voice, while also staying authentic to how you speak. We do not need to change our voices to achieve a special "meditation" voice. We should speak as we naturally do, so long as we deliver the guidance slowly and clearly.

- **Incorporating invitational language:** As we do throughout teaching and facilitation, we should remain trauma- and resilience-informed when guiding formal practices, using invitational language instead of commands.

    - ✓ "Let's now take a few rounds of slow and deep breaths"; "If comfortable, think of a time . . . "; "I invite you to reflect . . . "

    - ✗ "Take deep breaths"; "Think about a time . . . "; "Reflect on . . . "

- **Using your own language:** We strongly encourage you not to read from a script, word for word. This makes it easier to connect with the practice and deliver it more authentically. A good option is to prepare an outline, based on the script, creating brief summary headings for each section. For example: (1) Posture, (2) Settling, etc. Use the words that are meaningful to you. Have this list as a reference for yourself. If you are going to read word for word, which may be helpful at the beginning of your training, practice reading a sentence silently to yourself, and then looking away from the script and saying that sentence aloud. Then, do the same with the next sentence. This will help the guidance to feel more spontaneous and sincere. Though perhaps difficult at first, this will get much easier with practice and is worth learning to do.

- **Staying true to the practice:** While it is helpful to use your own words, it is also important that we not stray from the key elements of the practice and not replace invitational language or important instructions. This is an example of finding the balance between adaptation and fidelity. Please refer to page 38 for more information on striking that balance.

- ❋ **Original script:** "To settle into the present experience, let's take a few rounds of slow and deep breaths. As we inhale . . . noticing the nourishing air that is energizing our entire being. As we exhale . . . breathing out any tensions or worries. Allowing our bodies and minds to further settle into a calm and relaxed state with each breath."

- ✓ **Possible adaptation:** "To further calm our bodies and minds, I invite you to take a few deep breaths, slowly inhaling through the nostrils, filling the body with air. As we exhale, we can imagine we are releasing any tightness or tension in the body or mind—just letting that go with each out-breath."

- ✗ **No longer represents CBCT:** "As we settle into this space, breathe in loving kindness. Fill your heart with warmth and love. Breath out negative energy. Allow yourself to connect more with your soul and your true being with each breath."

- **Pacing:** Pacing is important when guiding meditations. Knowing when to add pauses and leave space for participants to reflect on the prompt is important. That being said, it will not be perfect for every participant—some participants like more space than others. It can help to change it up each time you lead a practice. It also helps to let people know that they can always tune out the guidance and self-guide if that is more helpful for them.

- **Engaging in the practice yourself:** Consider setting your own silent intention/dedication before beginning to remind yourself that this is a gift for others, and that part of your task is to accept your level of experience, whatever it may be, and do as well as you can for the sake of the practitioner. If you are more familiar with leading meditation, then you can focus on relaxing into the process, finding that balance between experiencing the practice and leading it.

Debrief and Takeaway

Refer to the "Skills for Leading Activities", Debrief and Takeaway section on pages 28–32 for explanations of the following skills, which also apply to facilitating the debrief and takeaway following a meditation practice:

- Uses language that is open and non-presumptive [page 28]

- Asks open-ended questions [page 29]

- Knows when to listen, when to let others respond, and when to jump in and respond [page 29]

- Uses active listening and non-judgmental language to gain clarity on what participants are sharing and to affirm differences of opinions and responses from the group [page 29]

- Reinforces and clarifies content and redirects the class when a participant or group goes off-topic [page 30]

- Pays attention to the group's dynamics and learners' energy, attention levels, comprehension, and emotions [page 31]

- Attunes to participant engagement and provides opportunities for all voices to be heard [page 31]

- Manages challenging situations [page 32]

- Summarizes key points clearly and succinctly [page 32]

Fidelity and Adaptation of CBCT

Teaching CBCT involves striking a balance between maintaining fidelity to the program and being skillfully responsive to the participants we are teaching. A CBCT teacher is expected to make small additions to the official program—such as bringing new stories or modified activities, presentation slides, or novel ways of expressing the ideas—to communicate well with diverse populations while simultaneously maintaining fidelity to the core content and approach. That said, such additions are not considered to be new CBCT materials and cannot be posted publicly or shared beyond the specific CBCT class in which they are used. The core CBCT content and pedagogy, as well as the copyrighted materials, may not be changed, even as the method for presenting them evolves or shifts. Finding this balance will be covered in the Teacher Certification program, but when in doubt, please reach out to the CBCT team for clarity.

As you consider what adaptations may help for your audience, keep in mind that CBCT has already been formally tailored for several professional sectors, and any certified CBCT teacher can, after meeting any prerequisites and receiving a brief additional training, be certified to teach with these tailored materials. As of 2025, the following tailored programs are available:

Note: *Per the CBCT teacher agreement, CBCT teachers agree that they will not create new materials to adapt CBCT for a new context and will not translate CBCT into another language without written permission from Emory University.*

- CBCT for Healthcare Providers
- CBCT for Business and Leadership
- CBCT for Educators (aligned with the SEE Learning® (Social, Emotional and Ethical Learning) program)
- CBCT for Mental Health (designed for those taking CBCT from a mental health professional who is also a certified CBCT teacher)

CBCT is intended to be a universally applicable curriculum that does not promote a particular philosophy or culture. The Enduring Capabilities it endeavors to teach are considered beneficial to both individuals and societies. CBCT promotes the development of skills and insights that can provide a basis for greater resilience, wellbeing, and meaningful relationships between people of all backgrounds. With respect to CBCT materials, we recognize that cultural modifications may be necessary. Feedback on the written and online materials was sought from culturally diverse audiences to reduce the number of culturally specific examples and stories.

Still, there will be some parts that will need to be adapted to your context and culture.

You may consider the following ways to increase the cultural relevancy and authenticity of the program for your audience:

- Change examples that serve to illustrate key points to make them relevant to your participants' everyday experiences.

- Use your own stories when that modification will help your participants understand and relate to the subject matter. (But be certain you are clear on how your story relates to the content so that you are reinforcing a core CBCT insight, not just sharing a story that is personally meaningful to you.)

- Invite (but do not force) participants to offer examples from their own experiences and culture in a way that feels welcoming and safe.

- Listen carefully to people's answers to questions and remember the stories they tell, taking notes if you need to. As you get to know the participants, you can refer to their examples and integrate them into the sessions.

- When the language in the module seems culturally unfamiliar or not inclusive of your participants' experiences, change it so that it is not a barrier to learning.

Note: *Refer back to "Studying CBCT Content" [page 6] for a list of the key elements of CBCT. These are elements we do not want to adapt or contradict when teaching.*

A Special Note on Religious and Philosophical Beliefs

One of the most challenging aspects of becoming a CBCT teacher can be learning to disentangle one's personal philosophical or religious beliefs from the CBCT content. For most of us, there is much overlap between these realms, and CBCT certainly does not require or expect us to give up important beliefs.

For example, if we believe that all people have been created in God's image, that may help us relate to each person as special and valuable. If we do not believe in a creator God, we can rely on scientific perspectives, as well as personal experience, to infer that each person is unique and connected to us through the interdependent world we inhabit. As a teacher, we may feel strongly one way or another, but we make an effort to teach so that both belief systems are respected.

As a teacher who is interested in making the practices of CBCT accessible to a diverse audience, we want to be cautious not to impose our personal religious beliefs onto our participants, regardless of what tradition we are from. This might include beliefs in a creator God, a soul, or an afterlife, or beliefs in karma or reincarnation. While CBCT has roots in Buddhist psychology, and many of those who study CBCT may be familiar with or interested in those roots, it is important that we refrain from bringing Buddhist religious or philosophical beliefs into the course.

Examples of belief-based statements to avoid as a CBCT teacher:

- Everyone is essentially good, deep down. (Or: Everyone is essentially bad, deep down.)
- Namaste, Amen, or other religion-related expressions (unless you are certain that you are teaching to a group that shares the same religious identity).
- By clearing the mind, I can rely on my inner spirit to guide me.
- Our souls are pure and good.
- God (or the universe) has a plan for all of us.
- We all have our karma!

The Second Quality of a Teacher: Practice

Practice is another core quality of a CBCT teacher. This refers to the teacher's commitment to their personal practice and their understanding that the learning is lifelong and takes time and repetition to become more embodied. Practice not only deepens a teacher's skills and contributes to their own wellbeing, but it also supports their teaching, as their personal experiences can be brought in to motivate participants and promote greater understanding and insight.

The understanding that there is always more to learn also leads to humility and vulnerability in teachers, both of which are important for building meaningful relationships and trust in the group. We can always improve, we are not perfect, we are not distant, and certainly, not above our participants. This understanding leads to greater trust, connection, and bonding. The teacher's vulnerability also promotes a greater sense of safety in the group.

CBCT Teacher as Learner

A CBCT teacher reflects, learns, and grows with their participants. CBCT is a group experience that is facilitated and guided by the teacher but engaged in by everyone. Everyone contributes to the learning experience and the outcomes.

CBCT teacher training, continued practice, and the act of teaching itself deepen a teacher's understanding of the content and practices. While there is a level of expertise that comes with this, CBCT is a lifelong practice and does not depend on teachers having perfected any of the skills or insights to facilitate an exploration of the mental and emotional attitudes and skills presented in the program. This understanding can also relax expectations we may otherwise place on ourselves to always know the "right answers." There may be times we need a moment to think about a question being posed in a class. In those moments, we can thank the participant for the question and turn to our co-teacher if we have one, or open it up to the group to see if there is group wisdom that can be shared. We can also take those times as opportunities to consult the content and gain a deeper understanding of the material and get back to them at a later time. We invite you to experience the joy of being a learner and practitioner of CBCT!

Through the development of our personal practice, we deepen our understanding, develop new skills, and grapple with challenges and successes similar to our participants'. This learning journey provides common experiences that we can collectively reflect on and discuss. These common experiences can evoke empathy and understanding between teachers and participants, having a positive impact on our relationships in class. We might experience similar "aha" moments and appreciate the transformation that takes place through receiving knowledge and experiencing critical insights together.

As we commit to a personal practice, our understanding and skills will develop over time. The hope is that this will lead to benefits for ourselves, as well as an increased ability to facilitate similar experiences for our participants. Beyond that, our participants are sure to notice, benefit, and learn from how we model resilience, impulse control, non-judgment, compassion, and discernment—and how we highlight our humanity, including our imperfections.

The Third Quality of a Teacher: Warm-Heartedness

In the Tibetan Buddhist tradition, it is said that if you are seeking a teacher, the most important quality that they can have is warm-heartedness. Practice and warm-heartedness are deeply intertwined. The practice allows teachers to stay connected to their motivations to expand compassion and to deepen their compassion for others, including their participants in the course. With continued practice comes greater embodiment of warm-heartedness and compassion, which is essential to the teaching of CBCT.

Sharing CBCT in a meaningful and effective way depends on the teacher's genuine feeling of tenderness for the participants in the group, as well as the teacher's efforts to connect to this feeling and act from that place of endearment. The more we embody this warm-heartedness, the more it manifests in our body language, tone of voice, words, and actions, and this has a profound impact on creating a space of safety, kindness, and compassion, an environment in which learning can take place.

Applying CBCT Skills and Insights to Teaching

CBCT is a program that strengthens specific skills and insights to contribute to a meaningful life, centered on the warm-hearted connection with others.

The following section, "Applying CBCT to Teaching," reviews CBCT's Enduring Capabilities and how they can be used to support us as CBCT teachers. By strengthening each of these skills and insights, we can cultivate deeper and more inclusive feelings of warm-heartedness, supporting our embodiment of compassion. This embodiment enhances our ability to teach CBCT and to hold a safe, compassionate, and meaningful space for learning.

Applying CBCT to Teaching

Module 1: Connecting to a Moment of Nurturance

1.1 Attuning to one's sensations and feelings

- Connect to our own sensations and feelings before, during, and after teaching each class.
- Remain aware of our emotional state and the way it affects our role as teacher.
- Remain aware of where we are in the Zone of Wellbeing and notice when we are knocked into the high or low zone. Use resiliency skills for ourselves, as needed.

1.2 Accessing moments of nurturance to activate feelings of safety and comfort

- Access feelings of safety when dysregulated before, during, or after teaching.

1.3 Valuing being nurtured as a way to increase motivation to provide nurturance to others

- Connect to the motivation to be a source of nurturance, safety, and compassion for the group. Remain connected to the motivation to teach CBCT.

Module 2: Developing Stable and Clear Attention

2.1 Enhancing the ability to sustain attention on our chosen task, object, or experience

- Remain present with participants and what they are sharing or asking.

2.2 Increasing the ability to notice unhelpful impulses, emotions, and distractions

- Notice when distractions pull focus away from the class and its participants.

2.3 Strengthening our ability to disengage and redirect the attention where we want it to be

- When something in the class is distracting, redirect attention back to the goal (e.g., compassion, task, learning, participant sharing, etc.).

- If activated before, during, or after a class, apply the attention deployment regulation strategy, where we redirect our attention away from the stressor and toward something more pleasant or neutral for a few moments to help us regulate.

Module 3: Enhancing Self-Awareness

3.1 Enhancing awareness of the patterns of thoughts and emotions in our inner life

- Become aware of patterns that are helpful when teaching and those that are not. For example, we may have a helpful pattern to hold space for others when they are sharing something vulnerable. We may also become aware of unhelpful patterns, like wanting to immediately jump in to try to solve someone's issue for them. The awareness of these patterns allows us to continue engaging in the helpful ones and to unlearn the unhelpful ones.

3.2 Strengthening the ability to distinguish reality from our projections

- Notice when we begin to project onto situations in the class or what participants share, and consider whether this is accurate or if it is our interpretation that may not be aligned with the situation's reality. Approach situations and people in the class with "beginner's mind"—without preconceived ideas or judgments.

3.3 Deepening the understanding that thoughts and emotions are fluid and changing, not fixed or solid

- If we find ourselves stuck in a thought or emotion before, during, or after the class, we can remind ourselves that thoughts and emotions are fluid, and they come and go like clouds in the sky. This can soften our fixation or the distress that comes from the sense that these feelings will not change.

3.4 Increasing the gap between impulse and behavior, allowing greater choice and flexibility in our responses

- Notice when our impulses to judge or project come up, and make a point not to engage with them. This could involve responding to an activating situation with the regulation skill of self-distancing to get back to our ZOW, or it could be returning to a response of non-appraisal when we catch ourselves making a judgment of others.

Module 4: Cultivating Self-Compassion Part 1: Accepting Our Vulnerabilities with Kindness

4.1 Sustaining awareness that we are not alone in having setbacks and limitations

- Exercise understanding and kindness toward ourselves when a mistake is made. This could be if we forget an aspect of the content or class plan, answer a question in a way we didn't like, say the wrong thing, or lose track of time, among others. Remind ourselves in these moments that we are human, and mistakes happen to all of us. We are not alone!

4.2 Maintaining the broader perspective that, while we may have limitations and challenges, we also have strengths and opportunities

- Attune to our strengths as a teacher. Take time to acknowledge what our strengths are, what we are doing well in the class, and what else is going well, so that we do not get caught in a negativity bias and lose sight of the positives. This can be applied when looking back on a finished class and preparing for the next one, helping us have a more accurate and broader view, rather than a narrower lens, overly focused on what did not go well. Acknowledge that we might feel something did not go well, but others might feel differently. Be curious about what others' experiences were and are.

4.3 Applying a systems-thinking perspective to setbacks, understanding that there are many contributing factors to any outcome that are not all within our control

- Recognize what is in and out of our own control, and use this understanding when we cast harsh judgment on ourselves for something that didn't go as we would've liked in a class or with a participant. This reminder allows us to soften our harsh self-criticism and accept that we cannot control every situation or outcome.

Module 5: Cultivating Self-Compassion Part 2: Finding Meaning in Our Vulnerabilities

5.1 Sustaining the awareness that we can grow and learn from our mistakes, failures, and setbacks

- Take setbacks that come up when teaching (such as mistakes on content, struggles with facilitation, or challenges with participants or co-teachers) as opportunities to learn and grow instead of getting caught up in excessive self-criticism, despair, or feelings of helplessness. These situations are inevitable and without them, we would not be able to grow.

5.2 Using adversity as a way to clarify our core values and purpose

- If challenges arise during the course, be they with our teaching, a participant in the course, or something or someone outside of class, see them as an opportunity to reflect on our values, aspirations, and motivations. Encountering suffering in our work or personal lives can remind us what truly matters to us.

5.3 Enhancing sensitivity and compassion for others who share our experiences of vulnerability

- In CBCT courses, we get to know our participants through group discussions and sharing. As things naturally come up that we have in common, particularly the challenging experiences that we have shared, we can take this as another opportunity to connect with and respond to them with empathy and compassion.

5.4 Strengthening self-agency and fostering confidence in our ability to alleviate our distress

- If overwhelmed before, during, or after teaching, we can tap into feelings of empowerment and shift our attention to the skills, perspectives, or actions that could help alleviate our distress.

Module 6: Expanding Our Circle of Concern

6.1 Enhancing awareness of our unconscious biases, assumptions, and judgments of others

- Check in regularly with our own potential biases, assumptions, or judgments of people in the course.

6.2 Connecting to others by making our similarities visible

- Take time to find similarities between ourselves and our participants, and give them the opportunity to find similarities with each other to increase natural bonding in the group.

6.3 Expanding our ingroup through awareness that everyone shares the fundamental desire to be well and to avoid harm

- Recognize common humanity with participants: We all have the desire to be happy and healthy, we are all learning and growing, none of us are perfect, we are not above our participants, we are all on the same level when it comes to our common humanity. We can use these understandings to remain humble and deepen our connection to our participants. This sense of connection allows us to create an environment of inclusivity.

6.4 Increasing our capacity for acceptance, understanding, and forgiveness

- There may be times when someone in the class says something we don't agree with, or they may say or do something we find offensive. We can take this as an opportunity to distinguish the act from the actor and not reduce them to that thought, opinion, or action. We can also reflect on the insights from self-compassion, remembering that we ourselves are imperfect, make mistakes, and are more than any one of our actions. This can help us to soften toward that person and see them more fully.

6.5 Appreciating and respecting diversity and differences

- Appreciate diversity in the class, recalling the value that differences in the group can bring to class dynamics and learning. Respect different backgrounds, experiences, opinions, and beliefs. This also expands the sense of inclusivity in the class, embracing all in the group not only based on our common humanity but also through the recognition and celebration of our differences.

Module 7: Deepening Gratitude and Tenderness

7.1 Seeing that we depend on others for our needs

- Connect deeply to the reality that we depend on countless others to meet even our most basic needs. By embracing this, we model an other-oriented focus in the class and allow for greater opportunities for others to see and connect with this as well.

7.2 Expanding feelings of gratitude and tenderness toward the many who benefit us, directly and indirectly, through the awareness of interdependence

- Acknowledge the many ways our participants benefit us, directly and/or indirectly. Allow feelings of gratitude and tenderness for our participants to grow.

7.3 Appreciating the benefits of other-oriented attitudes and seeing the drawbacks of excessive self-focus

- Recognize the roles others play in our own growth as teachers. See the harms of excessive self-focus, and acknowledge that we are not the all-knowing expert and we didn't gain the wisdom and insights of CBCT all on our own. Our growth and understanding are the result of the efforts of so many (including, but not limited to, ourselves).

Module 8: Harnessing the Power of Compassion

8.1 Deepening awareness of the predicaments of those we hold with warm-heartedness

- Tap into the warm-heartedness we have already developed for our participants and consider their struggles and needs, both the things that may be obvious (like an illness, family struggle, or other setback) and those that are more hidden (such as a lack of opportunities, little emotional support, or views or habits that may not serve them well). Allow the natural feelings of compassion to arise for these individuals and sit with that warm wish and urge to see them free from those struggles.

8.2 Engaging the wisdom of systems-thinking to guide our compassion toward effective action

- Exercise discernment to best support the group. This involves being attuned to and learning the needs of the group, and then engaging in systems-thinking to uncover the many conditions that contribute to those needs, as well as our own leverage point (where we might be able to make a positive difference). As CBCT teachers, we also remain mindful of the ripple effect these practices can lead to. We may never know the impact we have as teachers, but it will likely be larger than we can see. This can feed feelings of encouragement, even when our actions may seem small.

8.3 Sustaining compassion in our hearts and through action

- Find opportunities before, during, and after each class to connect to our participants with compassion. Allow that feeling to become more embodied and expand to those outside of the class. This greater embodiment of compassion becomes clear to our participants in the subtle ways we speak, through our body language, and through our actions, and this is where we can have the most powerful impact on others, both in and out of the class.

The Third Quality of a Teacher: Warm-Heartedness

PART 2
Course Structure and Planning

CBCT Course Structure

The structure of CBCT courses is constantly evolving and depends in many cases on the specific teacher and context. This section illustrates a typical course structure when teaching CBCT with the digital platform, Compassion U. More information on the structure and planning of CBCT classes will be shared through the teacher training and resources page, and regular updates will be shared with certified teachers as new ideas and insights are developed over time.

Compassion U delivers CBCT through a combination of self-guided learning and live facilitation. The traditional structure involves nine live sessions that occur weekly with a certified CBCT teacher and other participants. Typically, participants begin the experience with the self-guided Overview module (one week prior to their first live session). In this module, they are introduced to compassion and resilience through insight activities and formal and informal practices. Once they complete the self-guided lessons of the Overview module, they are expected to attend a live facilitated session on the Overview. Participants then begin the self-guided experience of Module 1, and when those lessons are completed, attend a Module 1 live session. This process continues through Module 8 of CBCT. After the Module 8 live session, which is typically the 9th and final live session in the course, participants engage in a short self-guided module, called "What's Next", where they can reflect on their journey and receive guidance on how they can continue engaging in the CBCT practices moving forward.

Note: *In some cases, it may make sense to start the CBCT course with an introductory session to meet everyone and walk them through the Compassion U digital platform before they begin the Overview self-guided experience.*

What is Compassion U?

Compassion U is the digital learning platform designed to make CBCT available worldwide. The platform (web-based app) incorporates cutting-edge e-learning experiences and provides easy access to live sessions with Emory-certified teachers. Along with courses for the general public, Compassion U offers tailored programs for those working in education, healthcare, mental health, and business and leadership.

CBCT participants with a Compassion U subscription will have a profile with access to their e-learning course, resources (including guided meditation recordings, a journal, and more), and information about their live facilitated sessions.

CBCT teachers will be able to use Compassion U as both a learner and a teacher. Teachers will be able to track the progress of their participants (e.g., how many activities they engaged in, how many times they opened Compassion U, etc.). They will *not* have access to journal entries. Teachers will also be able to communicate with their participants through the app.

Certified teachers are qualified and permitted to teach CBCT without using Compassion U. However, when possible, we strongly encourage the use of Compassion U for several reasons:

- Users will have access to a library of meditation recordings and a way to track their usage of these meditations to help them build and establish habits.

- The content in Compassion U has been carefully crafted for comprehensiveness and fidelity to the program.

- If users spend their self-guided time doing activities, journaling, and learning the basics of CBCT, teachers will have more in-person class time to focus on answering participants' questions and to support the personalization and application of these new insights and skills to their lives.

- The app will be updated when changes or improvements are made, including new meditations led by new and diverse voices or with different lengths of recordings, etc.

- Users of the app will be able to learn about other Compassion Center events and resources as they become available.

- Using the app could help gather more data for research and better understanding the process, science, and benefits of compassion training.

CBCT Course Structure

Even if participants use the app for most of its features, some teachers may choose to deliver all the CBCT content and practices in live sessions, and they might instruct their participants not to engage in the self-guided coursework. In cases where the teachers choose to deliver the course without the self-guided portion, we still encourage participants to subscribe to the app to gain access to the meditation recordings (as well as the other reasons listed above).

Though there is a cost to subscribe to Compassion U and access the meditation recordings, the Compassion Center is constantly seeking ways to discount or provide scholarships to make the app affordable to anyone who wants to subscribe.

Component 1: Self-Guided

The self-guided portion of the course was designed by Professor Lobsang Tenzin Negi, along with the CBCT team and experts in e-learning. The aim of the self-guided experience in Compassion U is to ensure fidelity across CBCT courses and enhance the learners' experience with an engaging, interactive, and useful resource at their fingertips.

The self-guided element of the course will walk participants through all modules of CBCT, beginning with the Overview, going through all eight modules, and ending with a What's Next learning experience. In each learning experience, they will be introduced to the content and practices of that module—they will become familiar with the Enduring Capabilities, reflect through the insight activities, and engage in formal and informal practices. Their self-guided experience draws directly from the official CBCT Guide but delivers these key pieces of the CBCT protocol in an interactive and engaging format.

Component 2: Live Facilitation

Alongside this self-guided experience, participants of CBCT are expected to attend live sessions facilitated by certified CBCT teachers. These live sessions are integral to the CBCT experience. CBCT is, after all, a course about building connections. Going through this experience with others invites participants to tap into feelings of safety, form meaningful connections, and learn and practice on a deeper level. CBCT also focuses on the development of inner skills and habits at the personal, social, and systems levels. Certified teachers serve the essential role of supporting participants' vulnerable and profound experiences, as well as facilitating meaningful discussions and practices to reassure participants, clarify content, deepen understanding of the content, and offer an intentional space for greater learning in community.

Facilitation Structure of Live Sessions

Live facilitated sessions are led by a certified CBCT teacher. The typical structure, when paired with the self-guided e-learning experiences on Compassion U, is one-hour sessions that meet regularly (e.g., weekly or every other week). These sessions can be held online or in person. The sample structure presented in this section assumes that participants are also engaging in Compassion U's e-learning experiences, meaning they would have been introduced to the module and topics (and teachers would have been able to see their progress) prior to the live facilitated session. For those teaching CBCT without the self-guided portion of Compassion U, the structure and timing of live sessions would need to change to account for the need to introduce module content and activities during the class itself.

The sample structure for these sessions (illustrated on pages 60–61) includes the following elements: **Welcome**, **Brief Introduction**, **Deeper Dive Activity**, **Module Formal Practice**, and **Closing**. We recommend this sequencing when facilitating a live session, but teachers may choose to restructure these elements as they see fit to meet the goals and address the needs of their class. In some cases, a teacher may need to drop or rethink the timing of one or more of these elements in order to devote more time to another.

Live Session Format
(One-Hour Session Example)

WELCOME (~3 minutes)

- Welcome to this week's module/topic.
- Settling practice (2 minutes).
- Brief sharing of agenda for session.

BRIEF INTRODUCTION (~7 minutes)

- Teacher provides a recap of what participants did in the self-guided module, reminding them of the week's topic, the Enduring Capabilities, and key content.
- Teacher invites participants to share any insights or questions they have about the content, activities, or practices they engaged in.

DEEPER DIVE ACTIVITY (~30 minutes)

- Teacher leads an activity or discussion that aims to dive deeper into one or more of the concepts or practices presented in the module. There are three types of deeper dive activities: (1) Insight Activity Revisited, (2) Anchoring Story Reflection, and (3) Bringing the Skills to Life Reflection, outlined on page 61.

MODULE FORMAL PRACTICE (~18 minutes)

- Setup: Teacher briefly sets up the formal practice.
- Practice: Teacher guides practice on that topic, beginning with settling.
- Debrief: Participants share reflections, insights, and questions about the formal practice experience(s) they have had so far (in class and/or on their own).

CLOSING (~2 minutes)

- Teacher shares any final thoughts on the module and gives a sense of what is coming up in their next self-guided module experience.
- Teacher reminds them to engage daily in this module's practices.
- Teacher goes over any housekeeping items.

Facilitation Structure of Live Sessions

Deeper Dive 1 — Insight Activity Revisited

- Each insight activity focuses on specific skills or insights from the module. Any of the module insight activities could be brought into the live session to revisit and unpack.
  - **Choose insight activity:** Teacher chooses an insight activity from the self-guided module that participants were presented with prior to the session.
  - **Reflection:** Participants take time to revisit or modify their answers, or respond for the first time if they skipped the activity.
  - **Sharing:** Participants share insights and questions in small and/or large groups.
  - **Takeaway:** Teacher reinforces the takeaway of the activity.

Deeper Dive 2 — Anchoring Story Reflection

- Each module has an anchoring story that illustrates the module's key elements. These are found in written form in the CBCT Guide and as animated videos in the self-guided portion of each module in the Compassion U app. This activity gives participants more time unpack the story, gain a deeper understanding of its key content, and make the content more personal.
  - **Review module anchoring story:** This could be read out loud by the teacher or participants, or silently by each individual. Another option would be to show the video from the self-guided app again.
  - **Reflection:** Participants take time to reflect on the key elements of the module that are presented in the story, consider examples from their own lives that relate to the story, and think about how the key skills and insights highlighted in the story could be brought into their lives and what benefit that might bring.
  - **Sharing:** Participants share insights and questions in small and/or large groups.
  - **Takeaway:** Teacher reinforces the takeaway of the activity.

Deeper Dive 3 — Bringing the Skills to Life Reflection

- The goal of CBCT is to take the skills and insights from each module and apply them to our own lives in helpful and meaningful ways. This deeper dive activity gives participants time to deepen their understanding of the content and their personal connection to it.
  - **Review key skills and insights from the module:** This could be done using the enduring capabilities and/or informal practices.
  - **Reflection:** Teacher shares prompt(s) that invites participants to reflect on the value of bringing the modules' skills or insights into their daily lives.
  - **Sharing:** Participant's share insights and questions in small and/or large groups.
  - **Takeaway:** Teacher reinforces the takeaway of the activity.

Class Planning

Guidance on Co-Teaching

Co-teaching is not required, but there are many reasons that co-teaching is a beneficial way to offer CBCT (refer to "Co-Teaching Model" on page 14 for more details on this). Those who choose to co-teach will work together in planning, facilitating, and debriefing the sessions.

- **Creating a co-teacher agreement:** When entering into a co-teaching relationship, it is important to create an agreement together. This can mirror the group intentions activity (see explanation on page 24). It is often helpful to include a note to "assume best intentions" in the agreement as you engage in this work together. We may unintentionally do something to upset the other teacher. Returning to the understanding that we are both acting from good intentions can help us throughout the course and especially in those challenging moments.

- **Co-planning and coordinating:** When planning and coordinating the course, it is important to be on the same page. In some cases, a teacher may want to do even more than is required of a CBCT teacher (e.g., holding extra sessions, offering additional support, etc.)—these decisions need to be discussed and agreed upon by both teachers. To meet the basic requirements of teaching, teachers should work together to set expectations and divide the work in a way that feels right for the pair.

- **Different roles and responsibilities:** In planning, it may help to identify the different roles and responsibilities each teacher will hold. These may be responsibilities over the full course (e.g., one teacher is in charge of communication and the other is in charge of putting slides together). It could also vary per class (e.g., one teacher leads the meditations and the other facilitates the main insight activity).

- **Balancing who handles what in each class:** Each co-teaching pair decides who facilitates which aspects of each class. Regardless of what the pair decides, it is important that there is balance and no class feels overpowered by just one of the teachers. It is also helpful to switch things up throughout the course so that meditations or activities are not always led or facilitated by the same person.

- **Supporting each other:** The pair will determine a rhythm that works best for them to support each other and manage the class. This may involve an understanding that while one person was assigned to facilitate a specific activity, the other teacher can jump in to help if it goes off-topic or a question comes up that the facilitator needs help to answer. There should be a balance here, knowing when to jump in to support your co-teacher and when to take a step back to let them lead. This balance can be found through conversations between the two teachers and through trial and error.

- **Handling disagreements or conflict:** There may be times when disagreements or conflict comes up between teachers. When this happens, we can recognize it as a great opportunity to practice the skills of CBCT, particularly looking at our own views, emotions, or actions that may be contributing to the conflict, and the ways to shift that to contribute to a solution. If the conflict escalates, please feel free to reach out to the CBCT team at Emory for additional guidance. *Note: If disagreements between co-teachers come up during the class itself, it is best to wait until after class to address them.*

Teacher Preparation for Live Sessions

Step 1: Engage Content and Practice

Review content
- Read module chapter (including FAQ) in CBCT Guide.
- Revisit the module's self-guided experience in Compassion U to be reminded of the content, activities, and character journeys that participants would have just gone through before the live session. (Even if you are not able to look through everything thoroughly, at least click through it all for familiarity.)
    - It is especially helpful to see how the app's fictional teachers bring in content and respond to the characters' experiences.

(These will likely need to be brought up again during the live session.)

Engage in the module practices

- For the week leading up to the live session, focus on that module's meditation for your personal practice, and try bringing the informal practices into your life as well.

Step 2: Plan the Class

- Coordinate with your co-teacher (if you have one).
- Review the class plan, slides, and scripts for the module in the teacher resources page and make any necessary adjustments.
  - Review participants' progress to get a sense of what they have or have not completed. This can inform any adjustments you may choose to make to the class plan.
  - Consider pain points and common misunderstandings.

Step 3: Rehearse

- Prepare to guide meditation.
  - Consider what guidance you could share with participants for their formal practice.
  - Refer to the sample scripts on the teacher resources page.
  - Practice leading the meditation prior to the session. Do this out loud, perhaps to a family member (or pet).
- Practice what you are going to share during the session.
  - Rehearse how you plan to facilitate activities, deliver content, etc.

Step 4: Set Your Intention

- Immediately before teaching a class, it is helpful to:
  - Reflect on your intentions.
  - Connect to your compassion for your participants.
  - Engage in the settling practice.

Appendix A: Basic Descriptions of the Compassion Center and Its Programs

CBCT teachers are expected to have a general knowledge of the Center for Contemplative Science and Compassion-Based Ethics, its programs, and the Compassion Shift initiative so they can explain it to others and answer basic questions that their course participants may have. Teachers can also direct participants to the compassion.emory.edu website for additional information.

Lobsang Tenzin Negi, PhD, is the founding director of the Center for Contemplative Science and Compassion-Based Ethics and a professor in the Department of Religion at Emory University. Dr. Negi's research brings together his deep knowledge of Indo-Tibetan Buddhist and contemporary scientific perspectives to study the relationship between emotions and wellbeing. A former Tibetan Buddhist monk for 27 years, Dr. Negi received his Geshe Lharampa degree after completing his studies at Drepung Loseling Monastery in Mundgod, India, then earned his doctorate at Emory University. He is also the founder and spiritual director of Drepung Loseling Monastery in Atlanta, Georgia, United States. As Executive Director of the Emory Compassion Center, he directs the higher education programming; the CBCT program; the Emory-Tibet Science Initiative, which integrates modern science and contemplative monastic education; and SEE Learning® (Social, Emotional, and Ethical Learning), a K–12 educational framework and curriculum.

The Center for Contemplative Science and Compassion-Based Ethics at Emory University (Emory's Compassion Center) supports a research-based approach to educating both heart and mind. Guided by the vision of a compassionate and ethical world for all, the center develops educational programs, promotes dialogue, and engages in research to promote human flourishing.

Compassion-based ethics refers to an ethics that values and promotes an orientation toward kindness and compassion. This approach is grounded in the basic human values that can be discerned from common sense, common experience, and scientific perspectives.

Contemplative science is an emerging interdisciplinary field aimed at contributing to individual and collective wellbeing by providing insights into the nature of the mind and by validating meditative techniques for cultivating prosocial attitudes and traits.

The Emory–Tibet Science Initiative (ETSI)

ETSI is a unique educational endeavor, bringing together the best of the Western and Tibetan Buddhist intellectual traditions for their mutual enrichment and the discovery of new knowledge. These programs advance understandings of reality that incorporate both heart and mind with the goal of finding better ways to relieve human suffering.

CBCT® (Cognitively Based Compassion Training)

CBCT is founded on the premise that compassion is both innate and a skill that can be enhanced by anyone of any age, and it is never too late to reap the benefits. The most highly researched program of its kind, CBCT has been supporting the cultivation of compassion in adult populations since 2004.

SEE Learning® (Social, Emotional, and Ethical Learning)

SEE Learning brings the cultivation of compassion and other basic human values into education at all levels, from kindergarten up to university, through its age-appropriate curricula and rigorous educator-training program. Since its global launch in 2019, SEE Learning has shown that compassion can be taught to children in simple and increasingly sophisticated (and developmentally appropriate) ways.

The Compassion Shift® is an initiative of the center to advance a global culture of compassion through two educational programs—CBCT for adults and SEE Learning for children. This initiative aims to expand and make these innovative research-based programs accessible to people across the globe and especially to those working in the critical areas of education, business, healthcare, and mental health support.

Appendix B: CBCT Teacher Resources

The table below highlights some of the resources that can be found on the teacher resources webpage that you will be provided when enrolled in the certification program. *Note: This is not an all-inclusive list.*

CBCT Guides	- *Training Compassion: The Official Guide to CBCT®* (along with the tailored versions for educators, healthcare providers, business and leadership, and mental health) - *The CBCT® Teacher Guide* - The CBCT implementation guides (for educators, healthcare providers, business and leadership, and mental health)
Teacher Agreements	- Teacher agreement (for individuals teaching independently of an institution) - Institutional license agreement information - Senior teacher application
Course Planning	- Sample course structures - Sample class plans for each session - Additional guidance on content and facilitation per module
Presentation Slides	- Module slides (e.g., self-guided module recap, activities, content, etc.) - CBCT Workshop slides
Recorded Classes by Senior Teachers	- CBCT course recordings from courses offered by senior CBCT teachers
Meditation Scripts	- Settling practice scripts - Module formal practice scripts
Compassion U Instructions	- How to set up a cohort-based course as a certified teacher - Compassion U FAQ

Printed by Libri Plureos GmbH in Hamburg, Germany